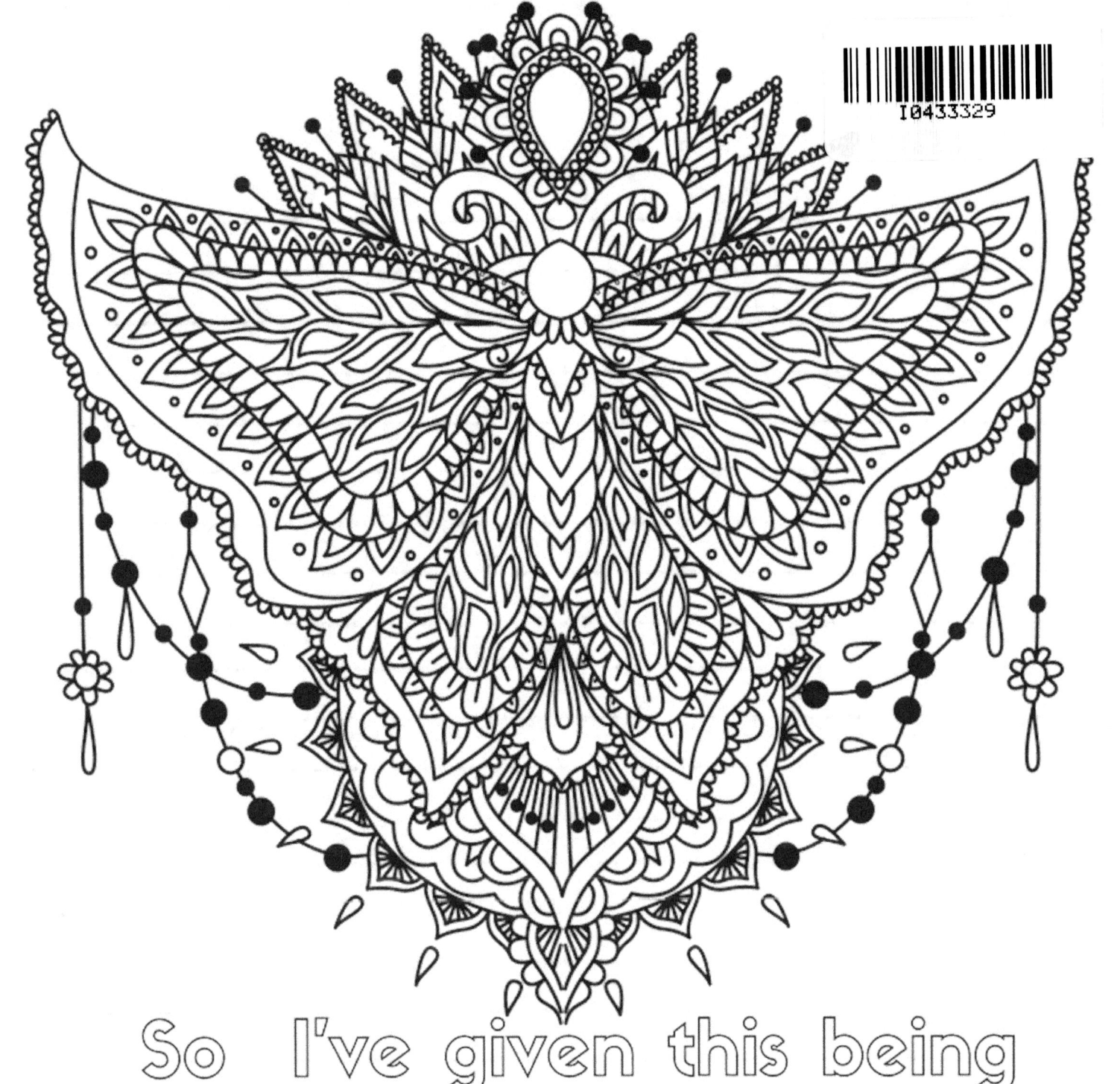

So I've given this being an adult thing a lot of thought, and yeah... I don't think it's gonna work for me.

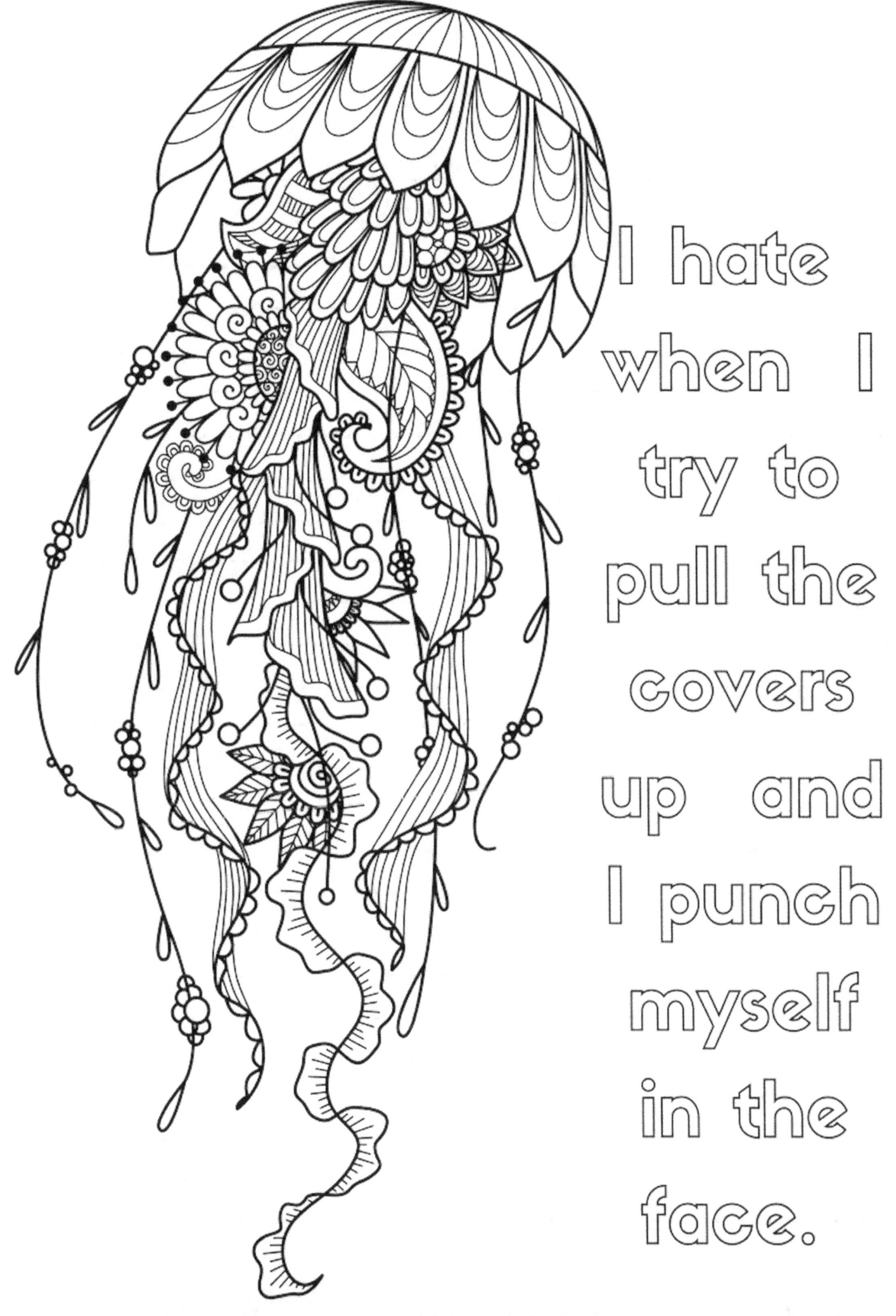

I hate when I try to pull the covers up and I punch myself in the face.

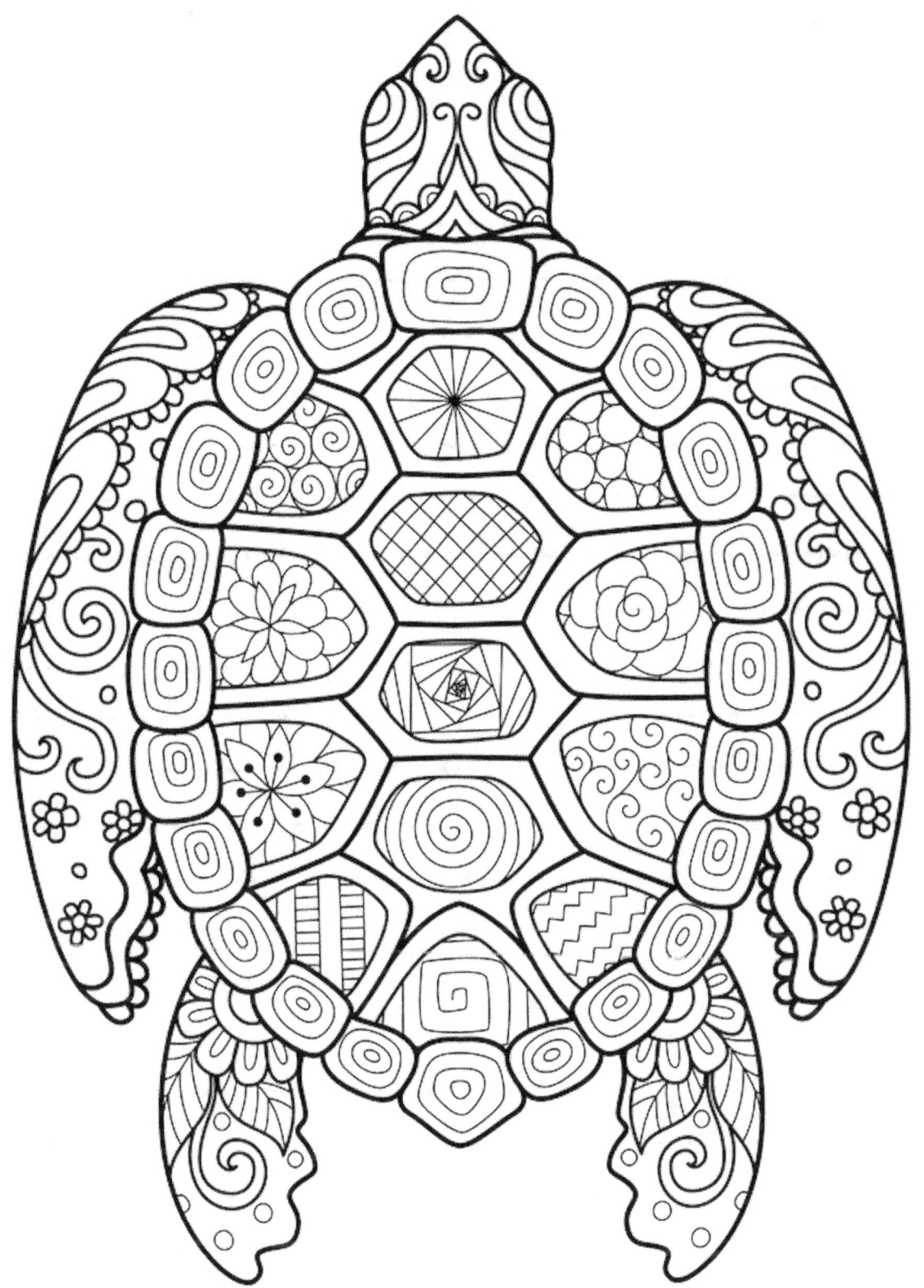

An apple a day keeps anyone away if you throw it hard enough!

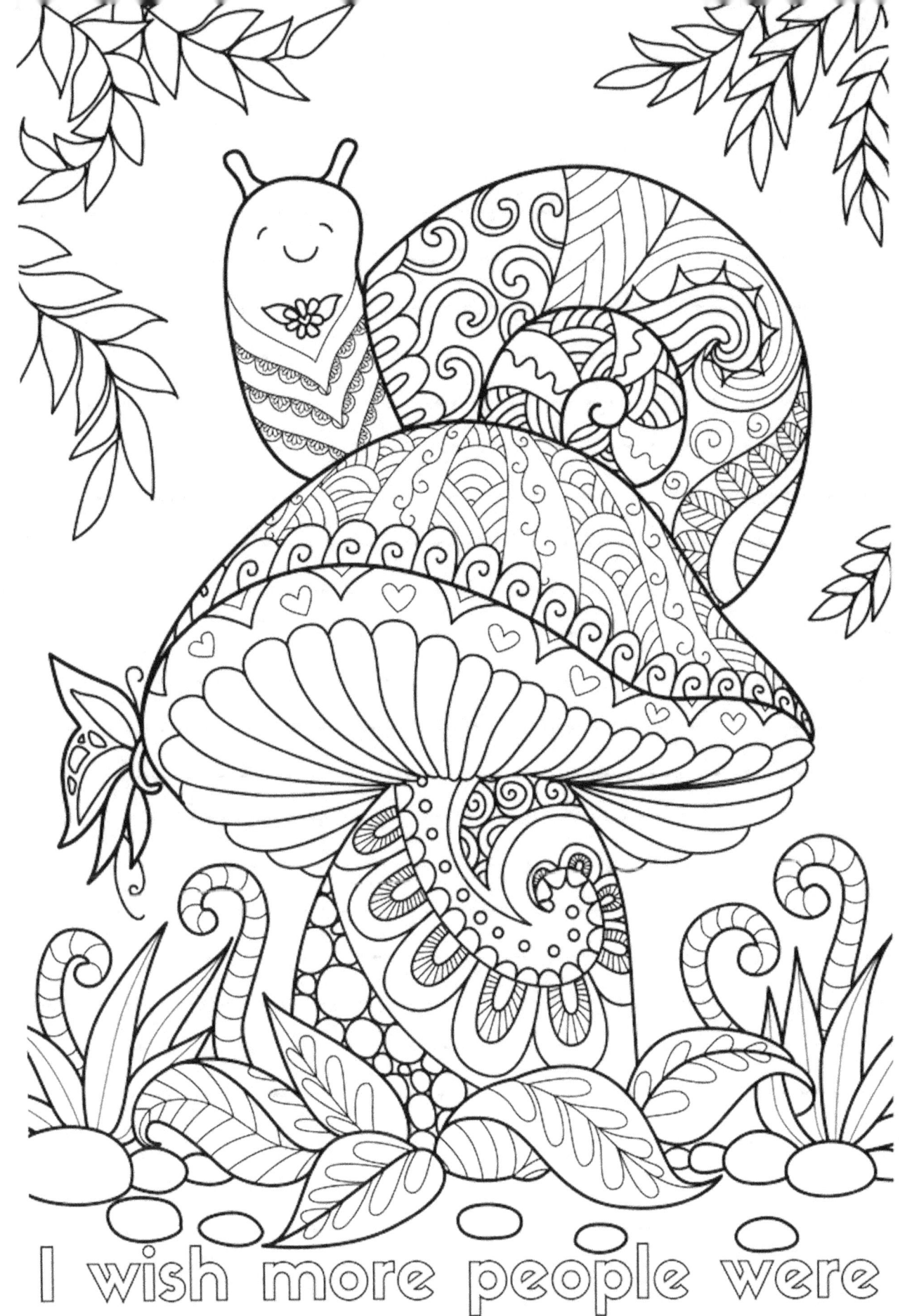

I wish more people were fluent in silence.

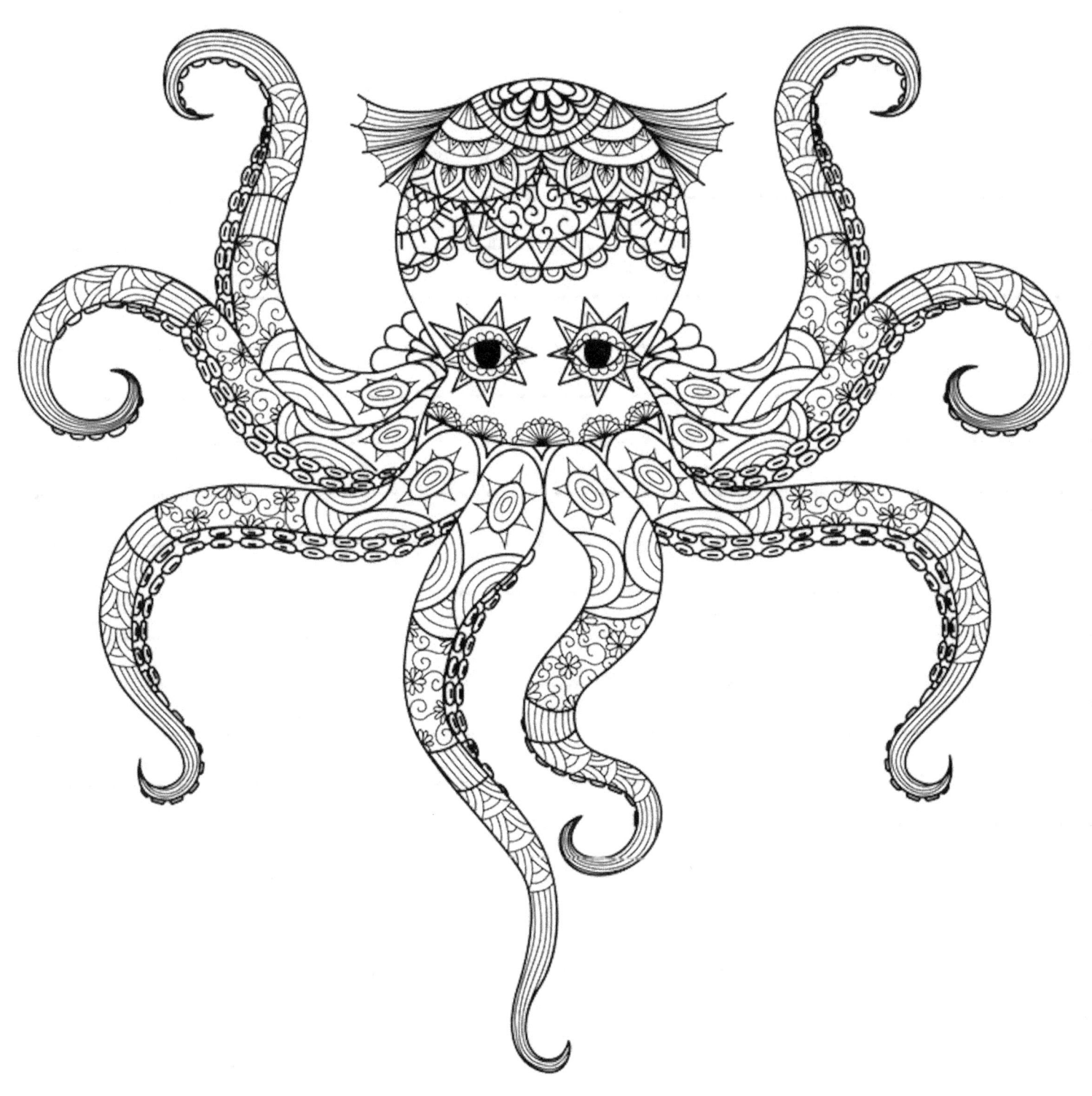

Be careful when you follow the masses... sometimes the M is silent.

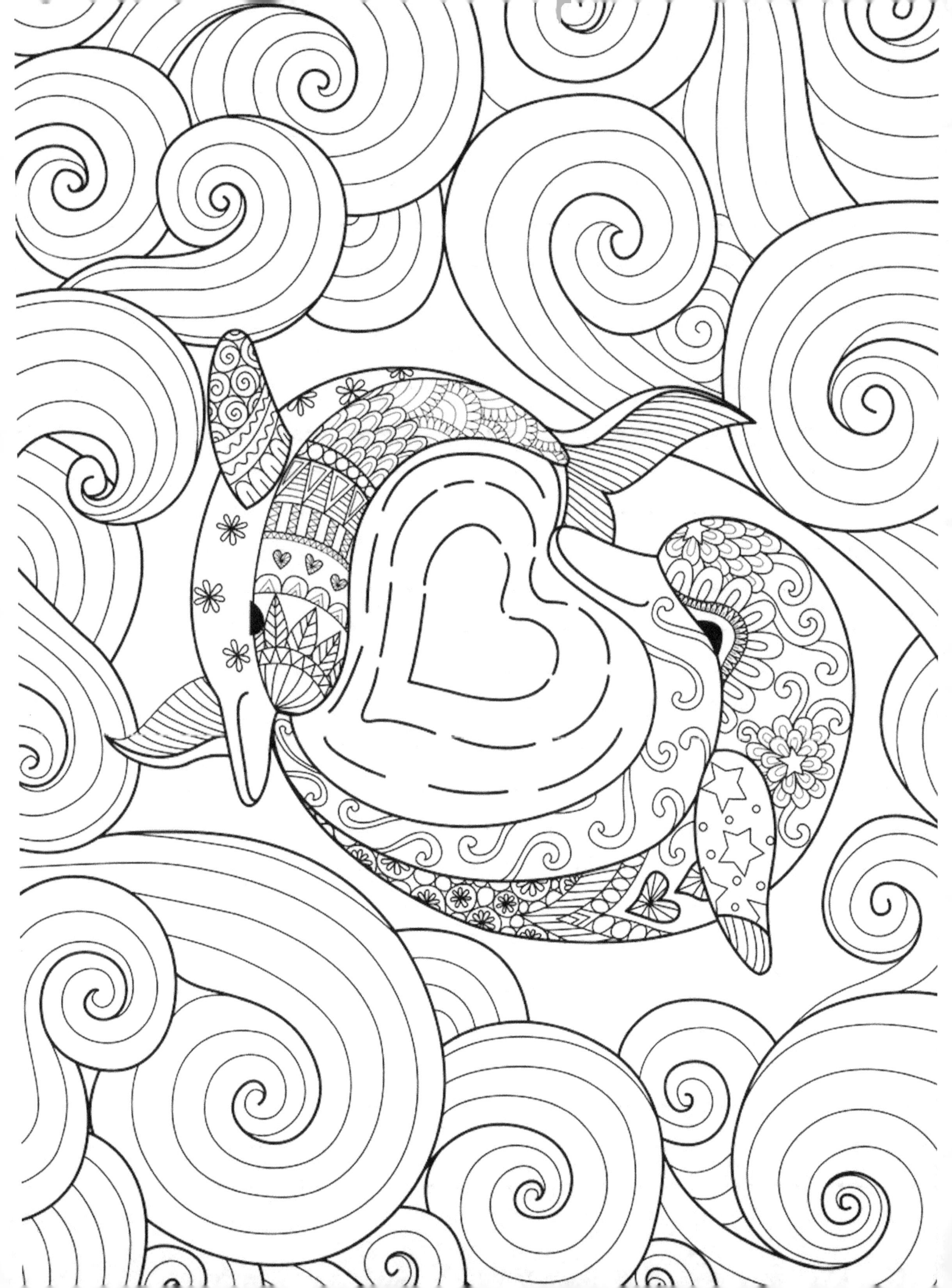

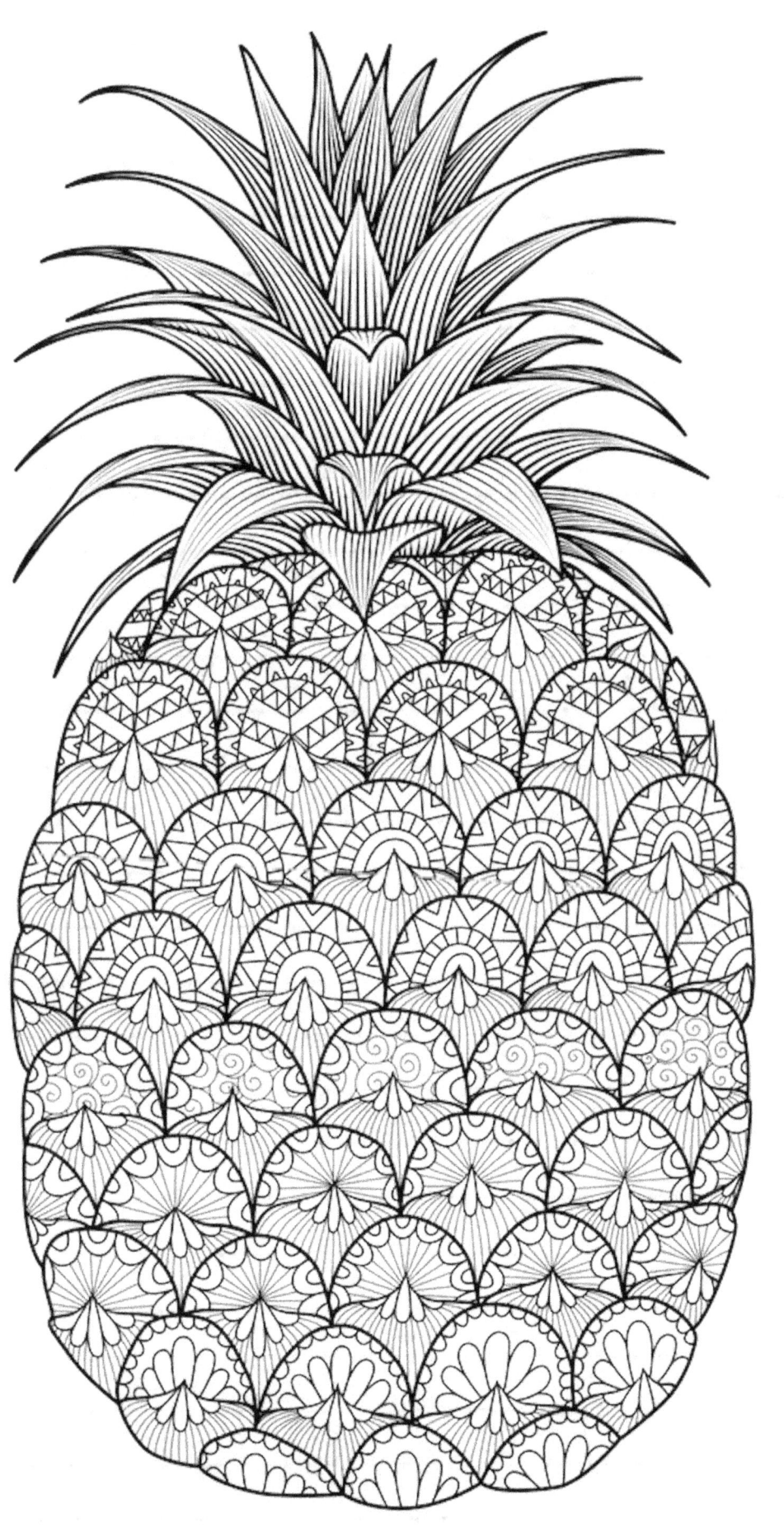

I have been putting a lot of thought into it and I just don't think being an adult is gonna work for me.

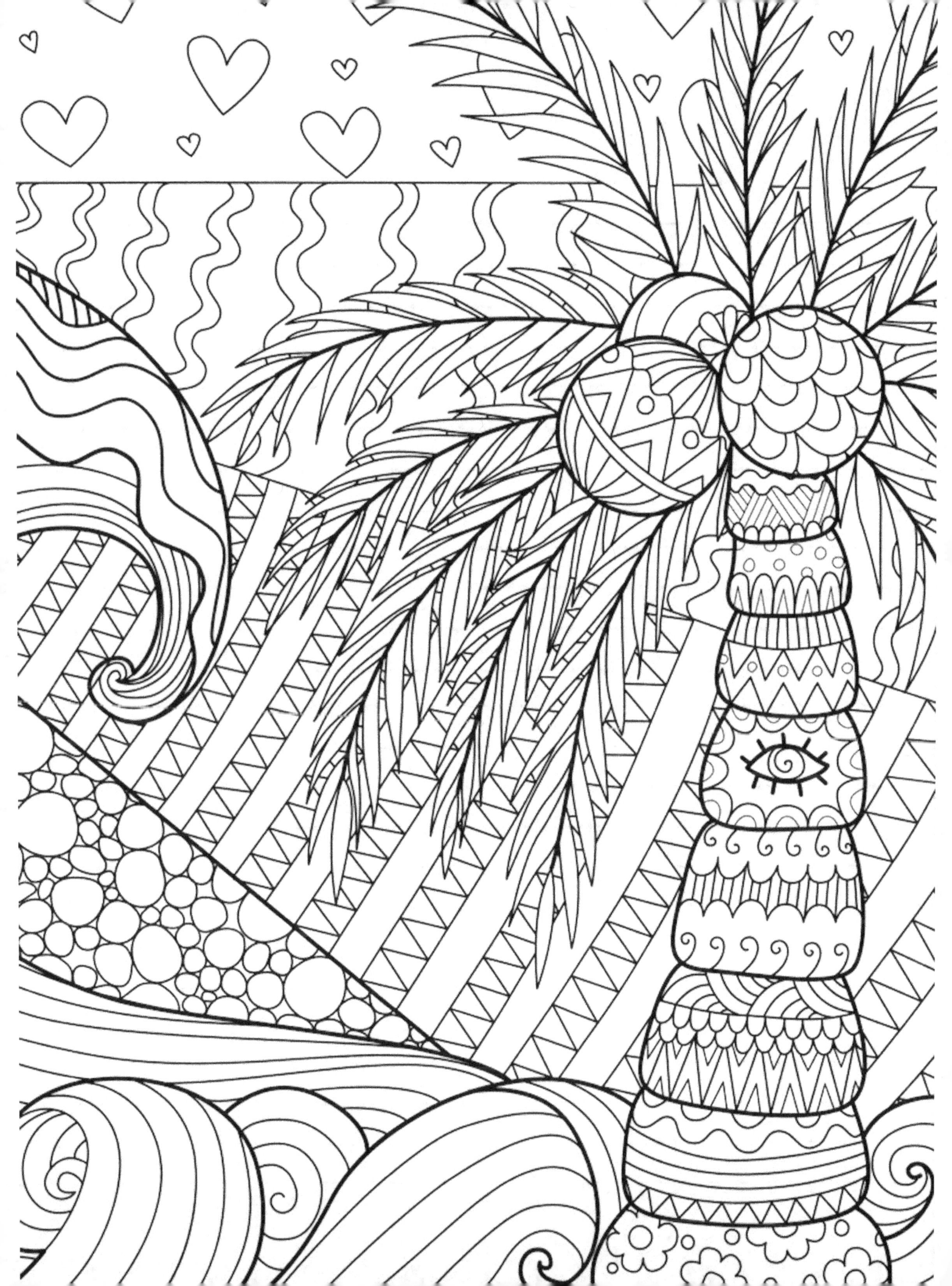

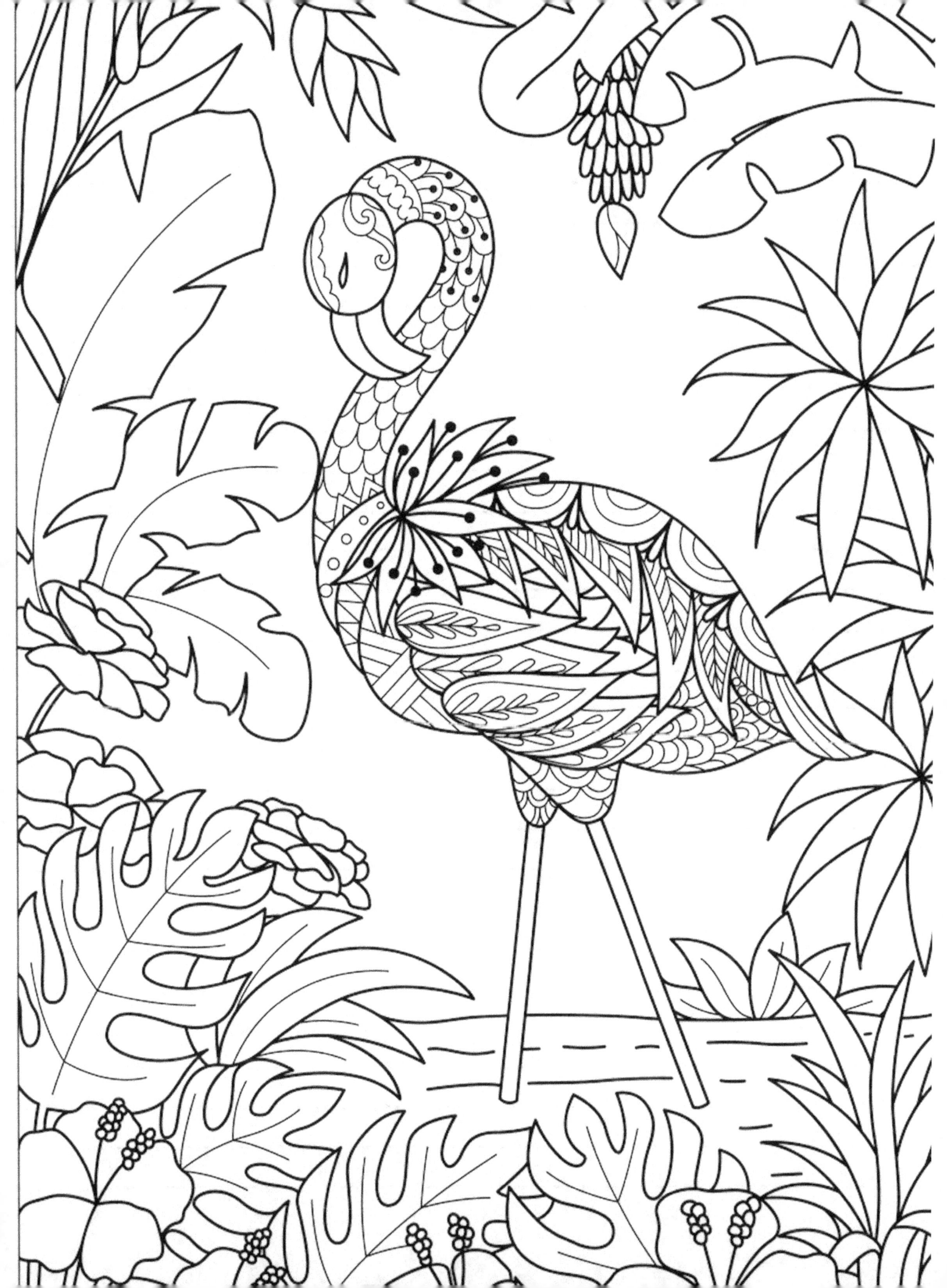

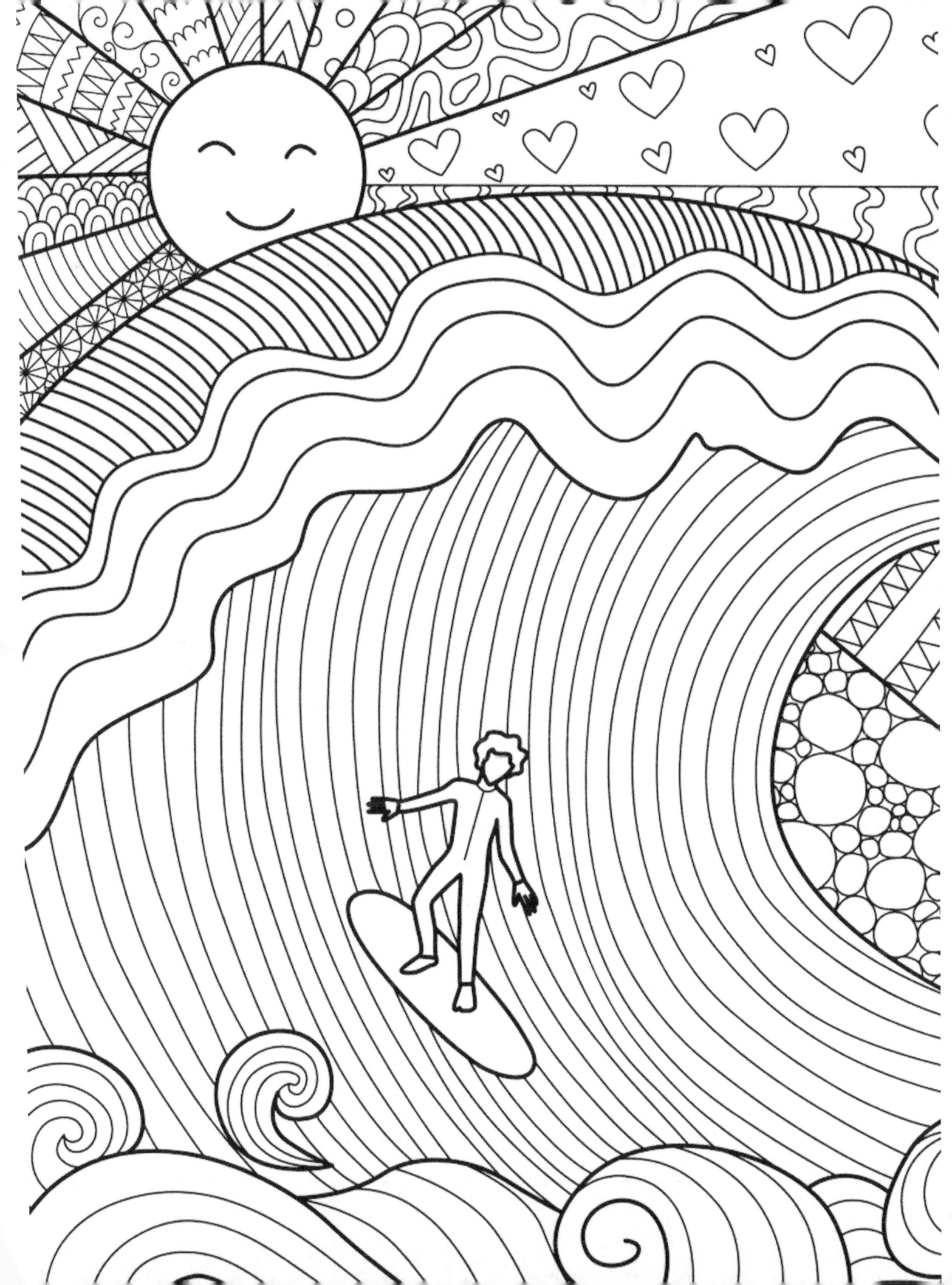

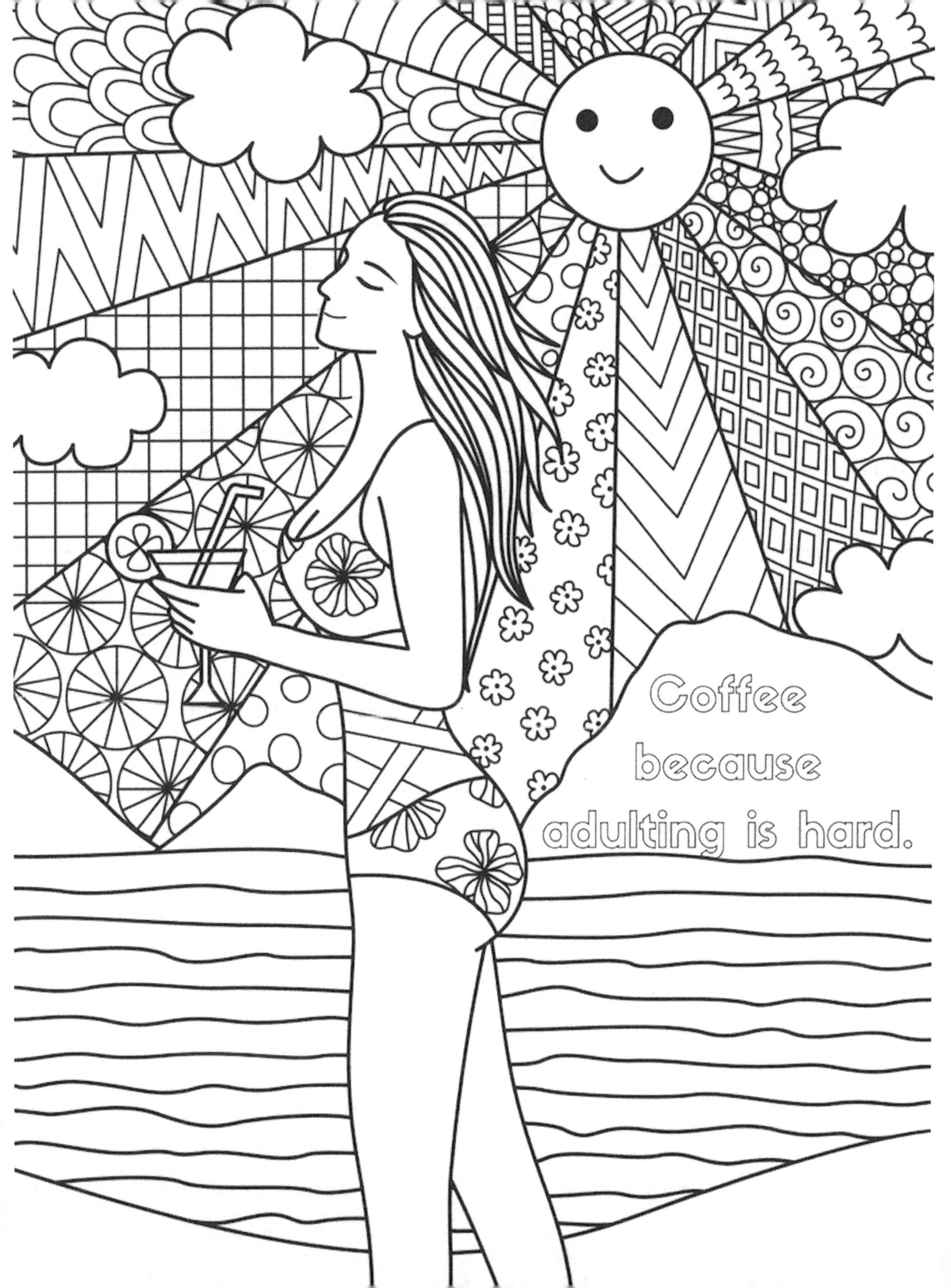

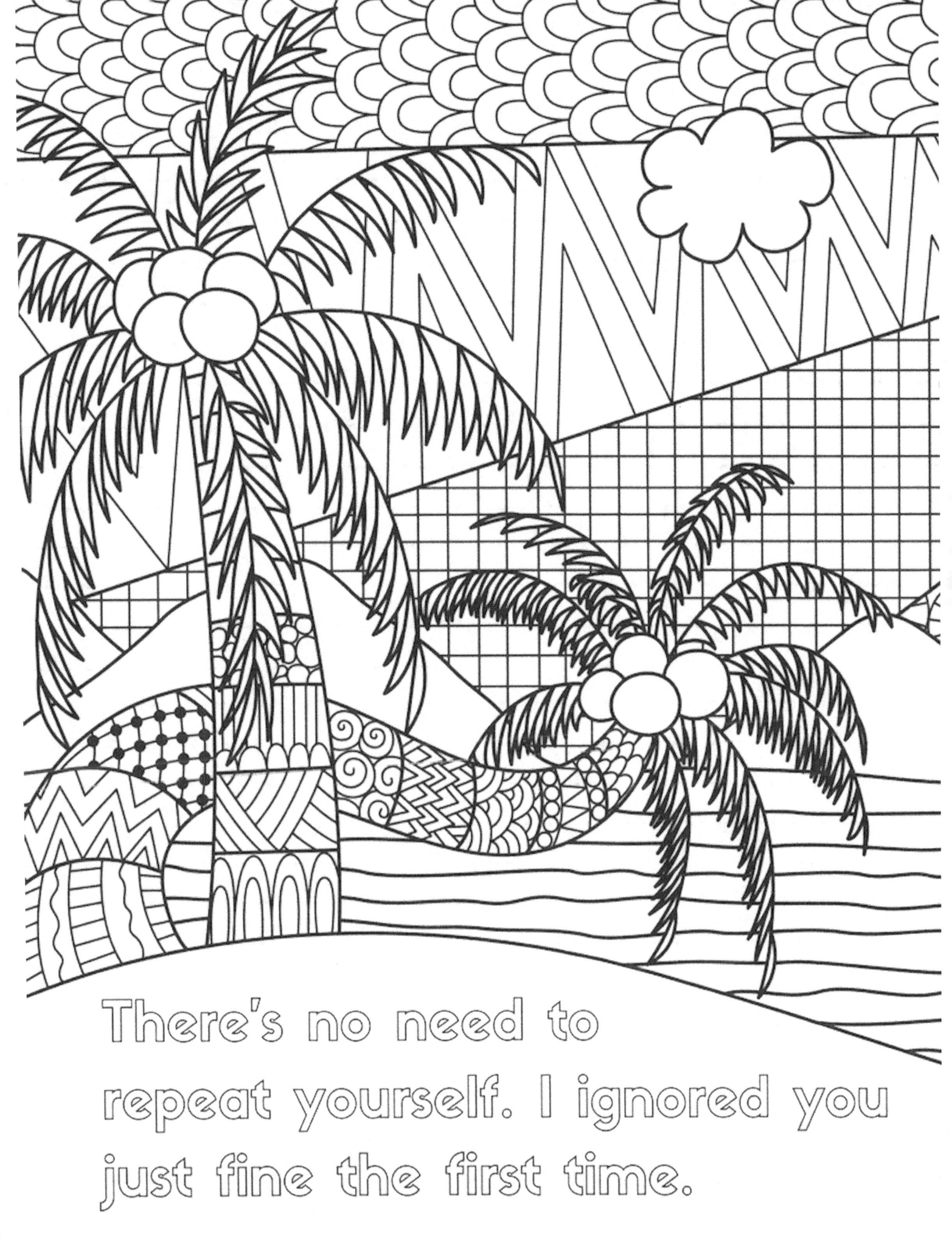

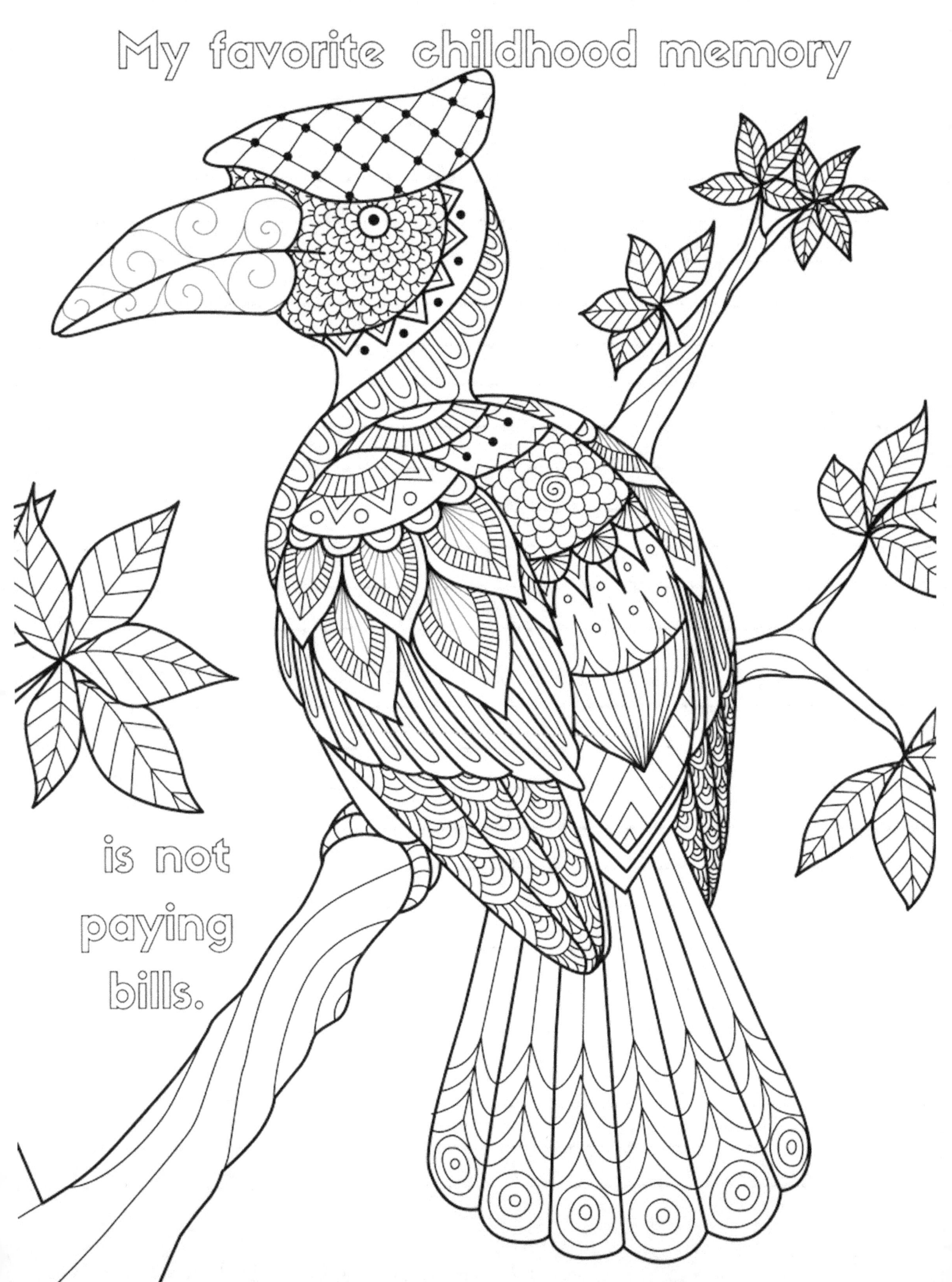

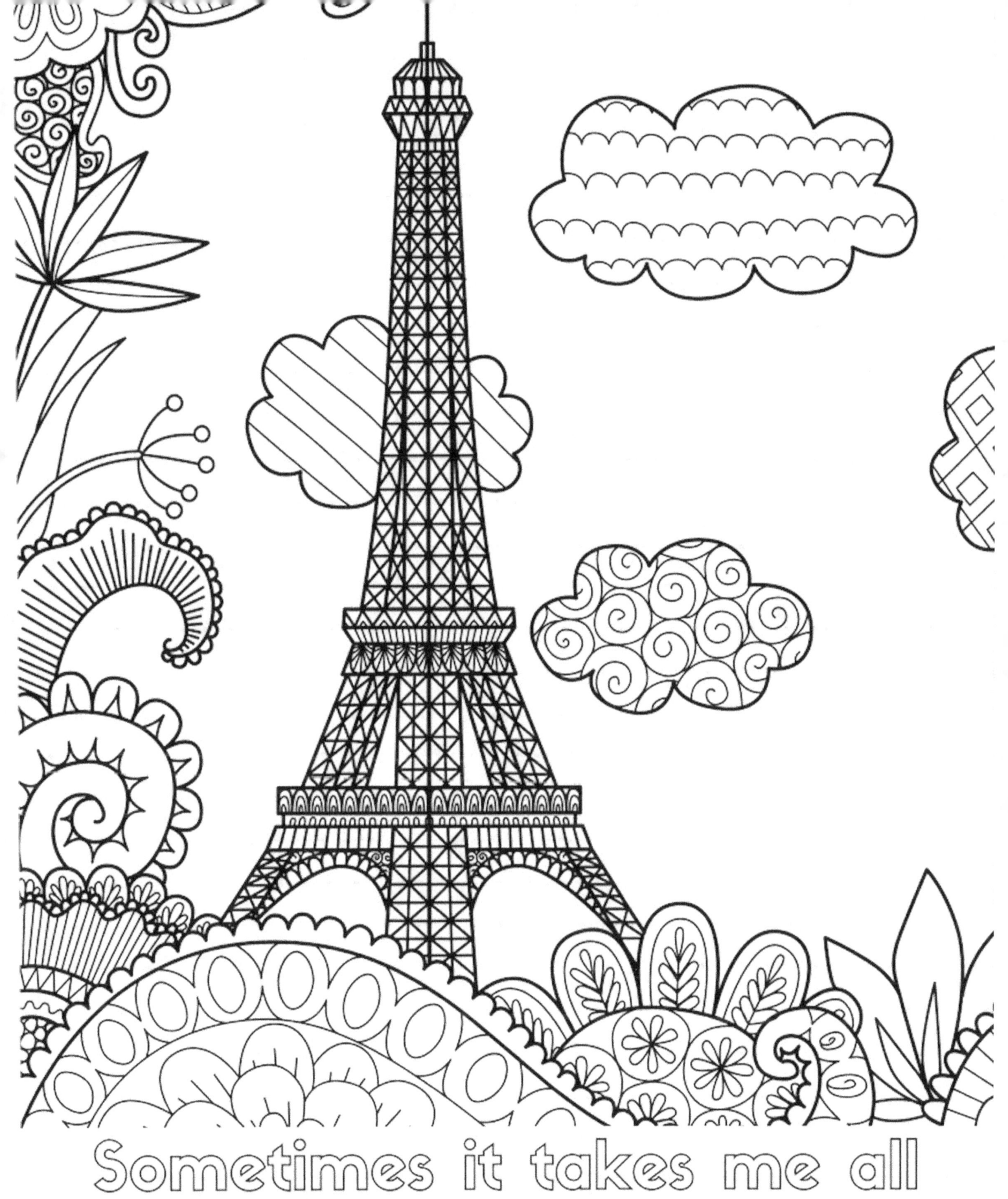

Sometimes it takes me all day to get nothing done.

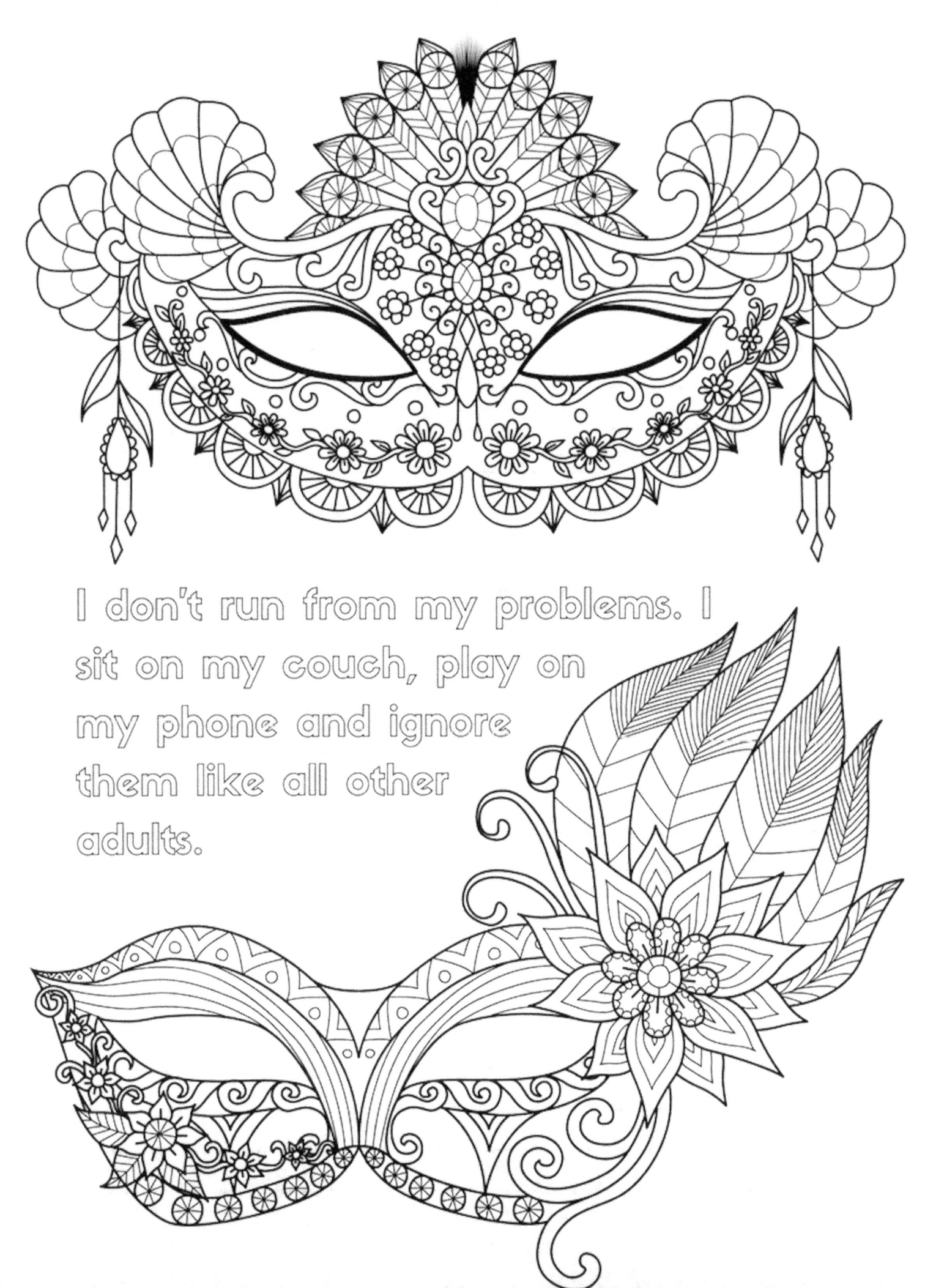

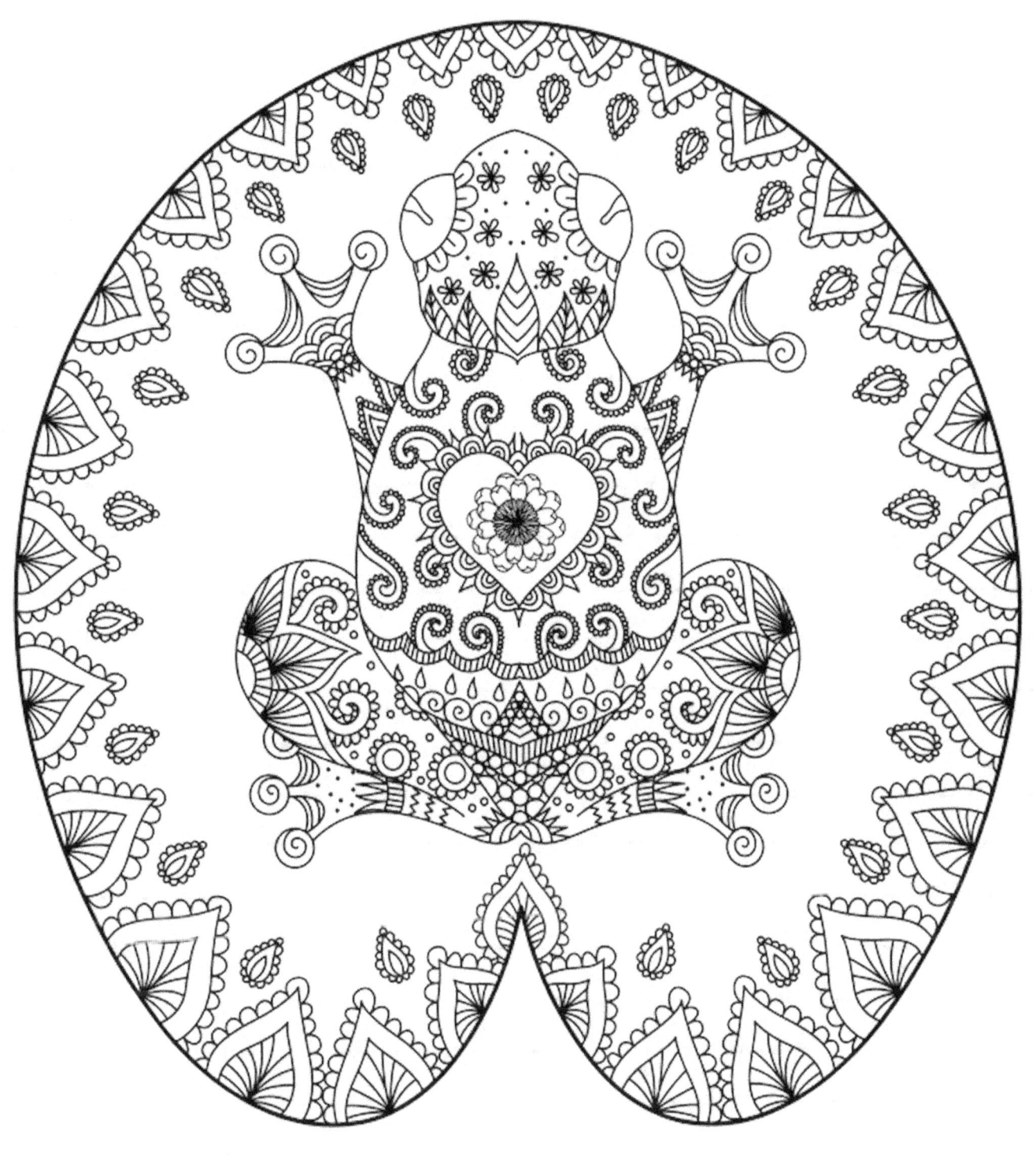

The first five days after the weekend are always the hardest.

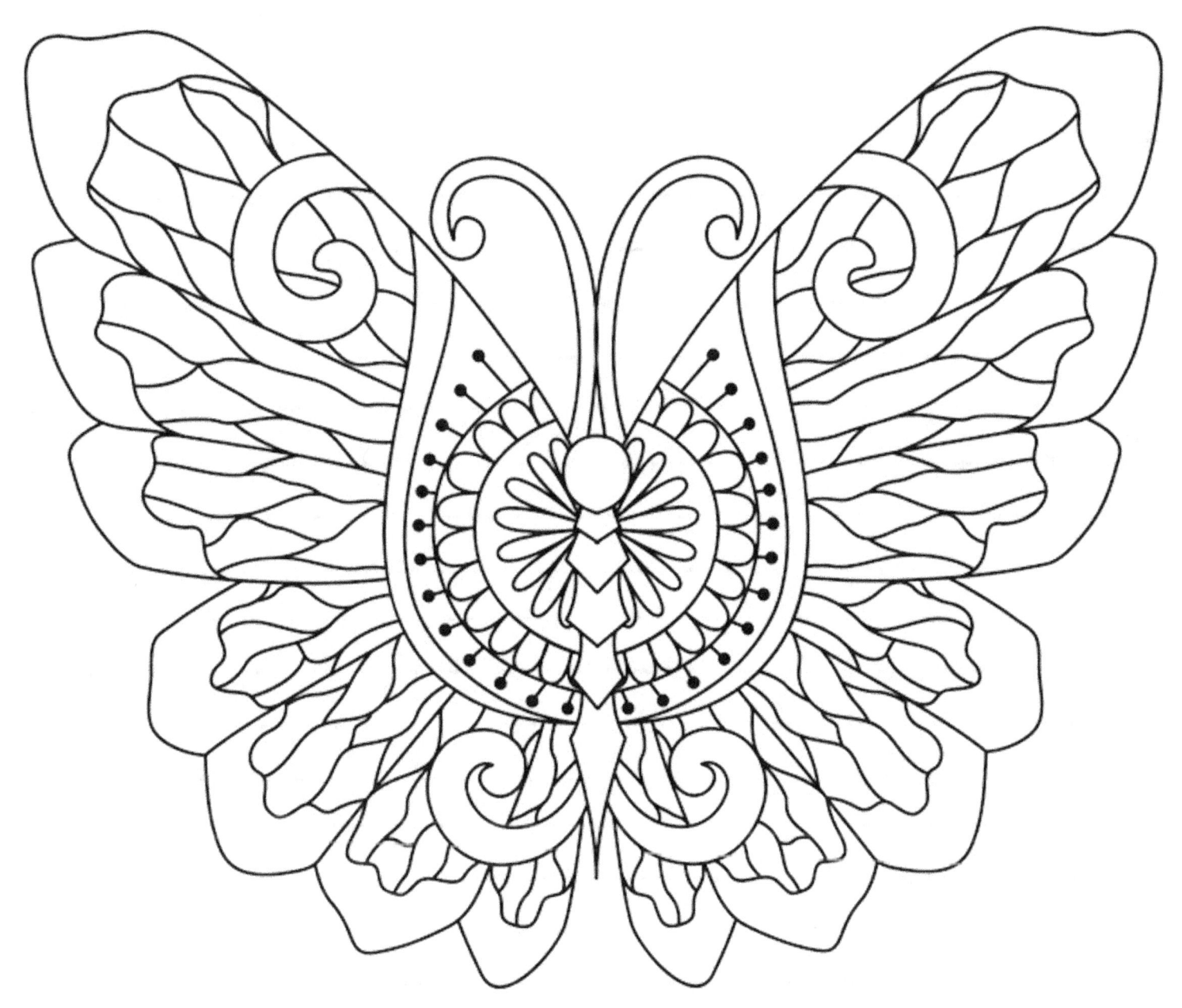

I wish all the extra fat on my body would fall off and turn into money.

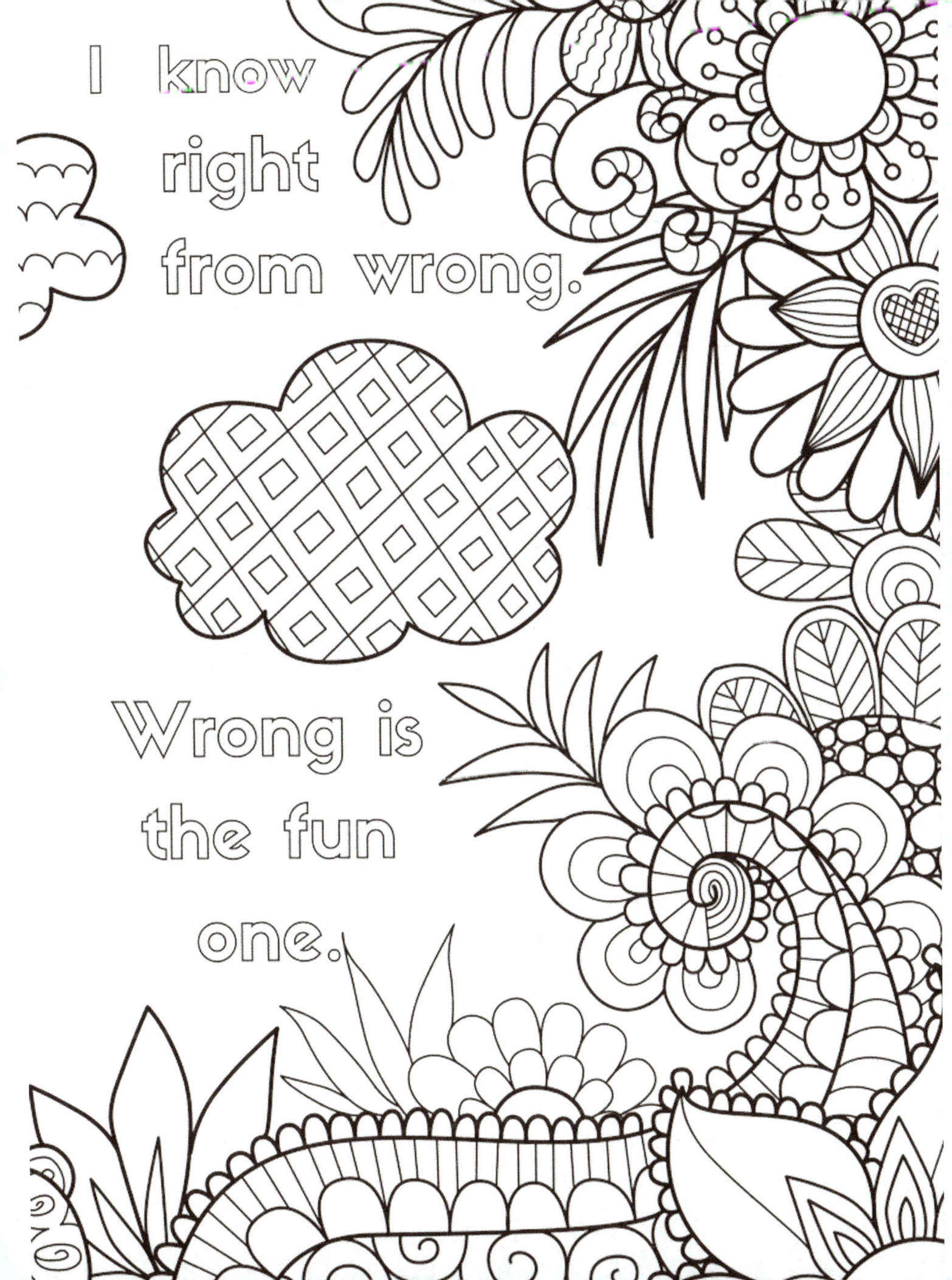

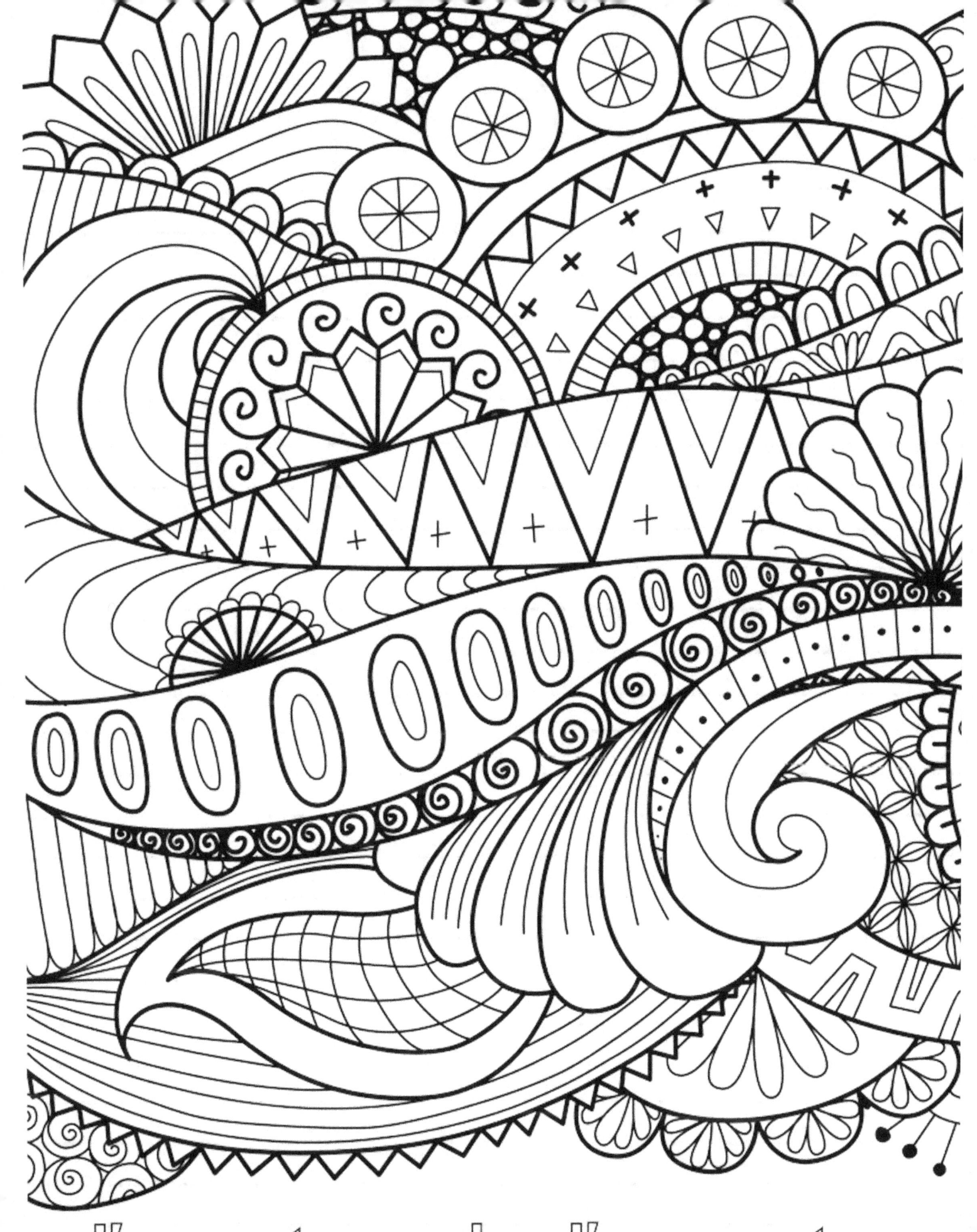

www.ingramcontent.com/pod-product-compliance
Lightning Source LLC
Chambersburg PA
CBHW082212220526
45470CB00010B/3143